www.neilhallam.com

Bobby

The Police Cat

Book 1

Published by Lauman Media and Publishing

Story Concept: Elaine Hallam
Written by: Neil Hallam
Illustrated by: Emma Walker

Cats Rule!

Bobby is a cat, but he is not an ordinary cat.

Bobby is a Police cat who lives in the Police Station.

He even has a Police Officer's hat.

Bobby does cat things, like chasing mice and eating the Policemen's sandwiches.

But Bobby also helps solve crimes.

Bobby solved his first crime the day he joined the police.

Someone left Bobby in a basket on the Police Station steps.

Bobby was having a nice sleep in his basket, dreaming about chasing mice.

Then, all of a sudden, someone very rudely woke Bobby up.

It was Burglar Bill, running away from his Police Cell.

OLICE

Burglar Bill tripped over Bobby's basket.

He fell flat on his face.

"Hey", said Burglar Bill.

"Meow!", said Bobby. Not at all happy at being woken up.

PC Joe put his handcuffs on Burglar Bill.

"Good cat", said PC Joe when he saw Bobby.

Hey!
Meow!

PC Joe put Burglar Bill back in his cell.

Burglar Bill was not happy.

Bobby went to the cells and looked at Burglar Bill.

“What?” asked Burglar Bill.

"Meow", said Bobby, sticking his tongue out at Burglar Bill.

PC Joe gave Bobby some fish as a reward.

"Meow", said Bobby, tucking into the fish.

“Where’s my dinner?” asked Burglar Bill.

PC Joe ignored Burglar Bill. Bobby ignored him too.

PC Joe knew that Bobby was eating Burglar Bill’s dinner.

Bobby had done a good job catching Burglar Bill.

PC Joe decided Bobby needed a Police uniform.

The Police don’t usually have Police Cats,

but PC Joe found something at the pet shop.

Doesn't Bobby look smart in his uniform?

Next day, Burglar Bill went to court.

Bobby went along to watch.

PC Joe told the judge how brave Bobby had been.

"Good cat", said the judge.

Bobby looked at Burglar Bill.

The judge sent Burglar Bill to prison.

“Drat that cat” said Burglar Bill.

PC Joe took Burglar Bill to his van.

Bobby led the way,

in case PC Joe did not know the way.

PC Joe drove Burglar Bill to prison.

Bobby fell asleep in the windscreen.

It was a very sunny place.

"Purr" said Bobby, as he dreamed about chasing mice again.

PC Joe patted Bobby's head.

There weren't any burglars to catch the next day,

so Bobby hunted the Police Station for mice.

Bobby was a very young cat.

He was better at tripping burglars than catching mice.

But, PC Joe gave Bobby a sandwich.

Today, PC Joe has gone out on his bicycle.

Bobby is sitting in the basket.

PC Joe cycled through the market place.

There was a little dog on the market place.

“Meow” said Bobby, as they cycled past the dog.

A robber ran out of the Post Office.

PC Joe gave chase on his bicycle.

“meow, meow, meow”, said Bobby.

PC Joe thought Bobby was a very good siren for his bicycle.

So did the people who moved out of their way.

The robber tripped over and fell on the floor.

PC Joe soon caught up with her.

Bobby jumped out of his basket.

He landed on the robber, with all of his claws out.

“Hiss”, said Bobby.

PC Joe put handcuffs on the robber.

He was very pleased with Bobby for being so brave.

PC Joe put Bobby back in his basket, and gave him some treats.

“Meow”, said Bobby.

“Oh bother!” Said the robber.

Now, the robber is in a cell, at the Police Station.

She isn't very happy.

Bobby has a bowl of cream.

Bobby is much happier than the robber.

"purr", said Bobby.

Today, Bobby and PC Joe are in the Police Station.

They are looking after the front counter.

A lady has lost her shopping bag.

Bobby is very interested in this case.

The lady had been shopping at the fishmonger.

Bobby and PC Joe are out looking for the lady’s shopping bag.

PC Joe is using his eyes.

Bobby is sniffing for fish, and getting very hungry.

Bobby sniffed out the bag behind a dustbin.

PC Joe is very pleased with Bobby.

Bobby and PC Joe are resting at the Police Station.

They have had a busy week of Police work.

PC Joe is eating his cheese sandwiches.

He isn't sharing with Bobby, because the lady gave him a fish for finding her bag.

What do you think their next case will be?

About the Authors

Neil Hallam

Neil is a freelance photojournalist based in Nottingham, England.
He contributes to magazines in: Australia, USA and Great Britain.
He is the author of several crime thrillers and non-fiction works.
The scriptwriters of ITV's Coronation Street, and BBC's Waterloo Road consult Neil over police technical matters.

Elaine Hallam

Elaine is a British Sign Language Communicator at Derby College.
Whenever possible, she specialises in animal care courses.
She is also the main proof reader for Lauman Media's output.
But Elaine is also a cat lover. Many of the mannerisms displayed by her cats; Nala and Tilly found their way into Bobby's story.

Emma Walker

Emma is Neil & Elaine's granddaughter, which makes Bobby the Police Cat a family project.
Emma is studying for a media qualification, and has become an accomplished illustrator and animator.
She is also a cat lover, and elements of her cat, Mr Binx's behaviour guided her vision of Bobby.

Printed in Great Britain
by Amazon

52295990R00023